Saint John
of the Cross
for Every Day

OTHER BOOKS IN THE SERIES

Saint John of the Cross for Every Day

Edited by
Kieran Kavanaugh, OCD

Paulist Press
New York/Mahwah, NJ

The Scripture quotations contained herein are from the New Revised Standard Version Bible, copyright © 1989, by the Division of Christian Education of the National Council of the Churches of Christ in the United States of America, and are used by permission. All rights reserved.

The text herein of the selected writings of John of the Cross is adapted from *John of the Cross: Selected Writings* (Classics of Western Spirituality series), translated by Kieran Kavanaugh, OCD, Copyright © 1987 by Kieran Kavanaugh, OCD.

Cover design by Sharyn Banks
Book design by Lynn Else

Copyright © 2007 by the Washington Province of Discalced Carmelite Friars, Inc.

Library of Congress Cataloging-in-Publication Data

John of the Cross, Saint, 1542–1591.
    Saint John of the Cross for every day / edited by Kieran Kavanaugh.
    p. cm.
    Includes bibliographical references.
    ISBN-13: 978-0-8091-4444-0 (alk. paper)
    1. Spiritual life—Catholic Church. 2. Catholic Church—Prayer-books and devotions—English. 3. Devotional calendars—Catholic Church. I. Kavanaugh, Kieran, 1928– II. Title.
    BX2179.J63 2007
    242'.2—dc22

                                                            2006029107

Published by Paulist Press
997 Macarthur Boulevard
Mahwah, New Jersey 07430

www.paulistpress.com

Printed and bound in the
United States of America

Contents

Introduction

Saint John of the Cross, born in sixteenth-century Spain, speaks with a vital timeliness. Distinct and contrasting traits sustain the enigma and the attraction of his personality. He was a contemplative and reformer, poet and theologian, troubadour of beauty as well as of the dark night, and a man both austere and kindhearted. John did not show any special interest in the spread of his written work. He did not promote the publication of any of his works; nor did he conserve his original copies, nor give them to anyone. Probably he destroyed them himself. John of the Cross foresaw a limited family of readers, and he became a universal teacher. He aimed at carefully hiding his person and his experience beneath lyrical expressions, such as "the soul," or beneath impersonal, doctrinal outlines. But this recourse did not work. He left his whole soul, life, and person more in the open than if he had composed an autobiographical confession. He offers a substantial and solid doctrine as he himself confesses. But in addition he has an existential core, and he writes with a deeply recollected spirit. He also possesses the sense of transcendence.

Because readers who dialogue with Saint John of the Cross are so many and so different, it is very difficult to know the themes that speak intimately to each one. He is a model of inspiration who leaves ample margin for preferences and lifestyles. Nonetheless, there are some essential points of his teaching that draw and instruct the majority. I attempt to give an approximate formulation of these:

1. God revealed and hidden: John is like a faithful witness to God who is both transcendent and close; infinite in his trinitarian mystery and close in his loving and merciful sharing with human beings.

2. Jesus Christ, the Word made human: Christ is the revealer of God

to us and of his word and gifts; the beloved who lives within, who gives and demands all, even unto the death of love.

3. Human beings along the paths of transformation: John speaks of humans with respect and love; and at the same time, he offers them both a plan of escape from their slavery and a life in keeping with who they are as children of God.

4. Faith, light in the night: God communicates himself in faith as he is, although by night; and by means of faith humans can take hold of the Presence in the revealed word, in history, and in their hearts.

5. Communion of love: We were created for love and in order to love; we will be examined in love. This was the key of John's personal life, and he used it as well as the keynote of his message.

6. Prayer and contemplation: By grace and vocation, he was a dedicated man of prayer throughout his

life. As a result he became a consummate master: faith and love, and keeping one's gaze fixed on Christ with loving attention.

7. Beauty: Beauty he writes with a capital letter because it condenses the being and attributes of God. John marvels at creation where God left persons and created things "clothed with beauty and dignity."

These attributes appear in all his writings. When he entered Andalusia in the south of Spain after his escape from prison in Toledo, it seems a rich mine was opened and he became a writer. Because of his experience and intellectual preparation, only one step was necessary for him to begin writing: the motive or occasion.

The motive for writing came quickly. The nuns in Beas enjoyed the depth of his poetry, his talks to the community, and his individual direction. They kept urging him to write these things down briefly. The written word would be an extension of his personal visits and living work. John became aware of the usefulness of such writing and yielded to the requests. He began leaving "little notes" with his written thoughts. "Read this often," he noted at the bottom of one of them. This was the beginning of his larger works. He became a writer without wanting to, without realizing it. He never wanted to be a professional writer, dedicated to concentrated study, to the preparation and actual writing of books. His works flowered in the midst of everyday life, prayer, suffering, and loving and serving his neighbor. In visiting the community of nuns in Beas, he did everything: heard confessions, dug in the garden, put up walls, laid floors in the monastery, and cleaned and decorated the altars. Taken together, the different activities of his consecrated life followed this hierarchy of values: religious life, responsibilities in government, spiritual formation and direction, confessions, other ministries, manual labor, and writing.

John was called to go further south into Spain. He entered Granada in January 1582 when he was forty years old. The six years that John lived in Granada amounted to his longest stay in any one place with the exception of Medina del Campo when he was a child and young man. He found in Granada an environment that motivated him to complete his greatest projects. In the midst of much commotion, he was able to create a mystical and literary work of the highest quality. Among his many duties at Granada was care of the discalced Carmelite nuns in that city. The special attention given to the communities of friars and nuns led to the writing of his major works that appear in the selected writings for the Classics of Western Spirituality from which these thoughts for every day are taken: *The Ascent of Mount Carmel, The Dark Night, The Spiritual Canticle,* and *The Living Flame of Love.* For information about the time and manner in which John of the Cross wrote these works, we have no better guide than Juan Evangelista (*Biblioteca Mistica Carmelitana,* editadas y anotadas por el P. Silverio de Santa Teresa, vol. 10 [Burgos: El Monte Carmelo], pp. 340–44), who helped him in both the business of government and the transcription of his books:

> As for what concerns my having seen
> our venerable Father write his books,
> I saw him writing all of them,

because as I have said, I was the one who was ever at his side. He wrote *The Ascent of Mount Carmel* and *The Dark Night* here in this house in Granada, little by little, for he wrote them only with many interruptions. He wrote *The Living Flame of Love* also in this house, while he was provincial, at the request of Doña Ana de Peñalosa; and he wrote it in 15 days while he was here with many other occupations. "Where have you hidden beloved?" *[The Spiritual Canticle]* was the first that he wrote, and he was also here; and he wrote the stanzas in the prison in Toledo.

Continuing on the same topic, Juan Evangelista makes some further clarifications:

I found that *The Ascent of Mount Carmel* had already been started when I came to receive the habit... and it could be that he had brought the beginning of it with him from there (el Calvario or Baeza). But *The*

Dark Night was definitely written here because I saw it.

The witness's observations about the unequal rhythm with which the writing took place are interesting: "little by little," "with many interruptions," "with many other occupations." This fact explains the limited amount of time the mystical doctor gave to his writing, and it explains as well certain defects in his work, which could have been corrected by a new, more careful draft.

The original works have not been conserved. The reason for this doesn't seem to be that they were lost, but that John himself did not want to conserve them. None of his destinées received the original copy of the work that was dedicated to them. All of them had to have a copy made. What is strange is that the author himself did not keep the originals. Where then did the autograph manuscripts end up? As a hypothesis, one might construct this process of composition. Fray John composed the respective work with a certain freedom: then he completed it, with annotations and corrections indicated in the margin. He next dictated it to some secretary or scribe who wrote it up in a definitive form. Then he tore up the initial draft as no longer necessary.

Saint John of the Cross's four great works come in a special form: each consists of poetry and prose closely connected. The same experiences or ideas receive simultaneously this twofold expression. His best literary and mystical creations keep his unbreakable unity of poem-commentary.

He wrote wonderfully in both forms. However the duality of expression was not the result of literary virtuosity. With recourse to this twofold expression, he sought in the best way possible to bring into relief the indescribable richness of the divine communication and at the same time, pedagogically, bring the reader close to it. He was mystic and master at once.

Previously two qualities were seen separately. In Toledo he wrote the naked poems, the symbolic and evocative poetry alone. During the El Calvario-Beaza period, he wrote sayings, maxims, precautions, and other brief things, all in prose. When he arrived in Granada with his thought fully matured, he fused these two means of expression. With these daily thoughts taken from the writings of Saint John of the Cross, I hope readers will experience something of the inspiration that John's first readers did when they kept asking him to write more for them.

January

Jesus also had been baptized and was praying,
the heaven was opened, and the Holy Spirit
descended upon him in bodily form like a
dove. And a voice came from heaven,
"You are my Son, the Beloved;
with you I am well pleased."
(Luke 3:21–22)

1
My help in all that, with God's favor, I shall say,
will be Sacred Scripture…the Holy Spirit speaks
to us through it.

2
The secret ladder represents faith, because all
the rungs or articles of faith are secret to and
hidden from both the senses and the intellect.
Accordingly, the soul lived in darkness.

3

It [faith] is an obscure habit because it brings us to believe divinely revealed truths that transcend every natural light and infinitely exceed all human understanding.

4

Faith, manifestly, is a dark night for souls, but in this way it gives them light.

5

The more darkness it [faith] brings on them, the more light it sheds.

6

This union [substantial] between God and creatures always exists. By it he conserves their being so that if the union should end they would immediately be annihilated and cease to exist.

7

This union [the soul's union with and transformation in God] is not always existing, but we find it only where there is likeness of love. We will call it "the union of likeness."

8

To love is to labor to divest and deprive oneself for God of all that is not God.

9

The preparation for this union, as we said, is not an understanding by the soul, nor the taste, feeling, or imagining of God or of any other object, but purity and love.

10

Perfect transformation is impossible without perfect purity.

11

The illumination will not be perfect until the soul is entirely cleansed, clear, and perfect.

12

Not all souls attain an identical degree of union. This depends on what the Lord wishes to grant each one.

13

Some see more, others less, but all see him and are happy owing to the satisfaction of their capacity.

14

In this life we may encounter individuals who are in the state of perfection and enjoying equal peace and tranquility, and the capacity of each will be satisfied, yet one may be many degrees higher than the other.

15

In this first stanza [of *The Dark Night*] the soul is speaking of the way it followed in its departure from love of self and of all things through a method of true mortification, which causes it to die to itself and to all these things and to begin the sweet and delightful life of love with God.

16

The soul states that it was able to make this escape because of the vigor and warmth gained from loving its spouse in this obscure contemplation.

17

It emphasized the intense happiness it possessed in journeying to God through this dark night.

18

So great was the soul's success that none of the three enemies (the world, the flesh, and the devil, which are always in opposition to the journey along this road) could impede it.

19

It should be known, then, that God nurtures and caresses the soul after it has been resolutely converted to his service, like a loving mother who warms her child with the heat of her bosom, nurses it with good milk and tender food, and carries and caresses it in her arms.

20

With no effort on the soul's part, this grace causes it to taste sweet and delectable milk and to experience intense satisfaction in the performance of spiritual exercises, because God is handing the breast of his tender love to the soul.

21

Since their motivation in their spiritual works and exercises is the consolation and satisfaction they experience in them...they possess many faults and imperfections in the discharge of their spiritual activities.

22

The wisdom and charity of God is so vast, as the Book of Wisdom states, that it reaches from end to end [Wis 8:1], and those informed and moved by it bear in some way this very abundance and impulsiveness in their words.

23

Who can describe the understanding he gives to loving souls in whom he dwells?

24

Who, finally, can explain the desires he gives them?

25

The Holy Spirit, unable to express the fullness of his meaning in ordinary words, utters mysteries in strange figures and likenesses.

26

The saintly doctors, no matter how much they have said or will say, can never furnish an exhaustive explanation of these figures and comparisons [in Scripture] since the abundant meaning of the Holy Spirit cannot be caught in words.

27

It is better to explain the utterances of love in their broadest sense so that individuals may derive profit from them according to the mode and capacity of their own spirit.

28

Mystical wisdom, which comes through love and is the subject of these stanzas *[The Spiritual Canticle]*, need not be understood distinctly in order to cause love and affection in the soul, for it is given according to the mode of faith, through which we love God without understanding him.

29

I hope that, although some scholastic theology is used here in reference to the soul's interior converse with God, it will not prove vain to speak in such a manner to the pure of spirit.

30

In all things that are offered to her [the bride], or with which she deals, she has ever before her that longing for her health, which is her beloved.

31

Since the palate of the soul's will tasted this food of love of God, her will is inclined immediately to seek and enjoy her beloved in everything that happens.

February

*Jesus answered him, "It is written,
'One does not live by bread alone.'"*
(Luke 4:4)

1

If anything pleases God, it is the exaltation of
the soul.

2

The property of love is to make the lover equal
to the object loved.

3

She no longer goes about in search of her own
gain and pleasure, nor occupies herself with
things and matters foreign to God.

4

She employs her intellect in understanding and carrying out the things that are more for his service.

5

[She employs] the will in loving all that is pleasing to him and attaching it to him in all things.

6

[She employs] her memory and care in what most pleases and serves him.

7

Her use of the body is now conformed to his will.

8

She does not rejoice except in God, nor hope in anything other than God; she fears only God and has no sorrow unless in relation to him. And likewise all her appetites and care go out only to God.

9

Before reaching this gift and surrender of herself and her energy to the beloved, the soul usually has many unprofitable occupations, by which she endeavors to serve her own appetite and that of others.

10

Happy is the life and state, and happy the person who attains it, where everything is now the substance of love.

11

The soul is not united with God in this life through understanding, or through enjoyment, or through imagination, or through any other sense; but only faith, hope, and charity (according to the intellect, memory, and will) can unite the soul with God in this life.

12

I desire to give clear instructions to spiritual persons on the narrowness of the way leading to eternal life—that narrowness of which our Savior spoke—so that convinced of this they will not marvel at the emptiness and nakedness in which we must leave the faculties of the soul in this night.

13

We can apply, then, what Christ says about the narrow gate to the sensitive part of the human person, and what he says about the constricting way to the spiritual or rational part.

14

Few there are with the knowledge and desire to enter on this supreme nakedness and emptiness of spirit.

15

This is a venture in which God alone is sought and gained, thus only God ought to be sought and gained.

16

It happens that, when some of this spiritual cross and nakedness of Christ's poverty of spirit is offered to them in dryness, distaste, and trial, they run from it as from death and wander about in search only of sweetness and delightful communications from God.

17

A genuine spirit seeks the distasteful in God rather than the delectable, leans more toward suffering than toward consolation, more toward going without everything for God than toward possession.

18

Oh, who can explain the extent of the denial our Lord wishes of us?

19

His Majesty taught this to those two disciples who came to ask him for places at his right and left. Without responding to their request for glory, he offered them the chalice he was about to drink as something safer and more precious on this earth than enjoyment [Matt 20:22].

20

These beginners feel so fervent and diligent in their spiritual exercises and undertakings that a certain kind of secret pride is generated in them.

21

Some of these persons become so evil-minded that they do not want anyone except themselves to appear holy; and so by both word and deed, they condemn and detract others whenever the occasion arises, seeing the little mote in their neighbor's eye, and failing to consider the beam in their own eye [Matt 23:24].

22

When at times their spiritual directors, their confessors, or their superiors disapprove their spirit and method of procedure, they feel that these directors do not understand, or perhaps that this failure to approve derives from a lack of holiness.

23

Embarrassment forbids them from relating their sins clearly, lest their reputation diminish in their confessor's eyes.

24

Sometimes they minimize their faults, and at other times they become discouraged by them since they felt they were already saints, and they become impatient and angry with themselves, which is yet another fault.

25

They dislike praising anyone else, but they love to receive praise.

26

Since they are truly humble, their growing fervor and the increased number of their good deeds and the gratification they receive from them only cause them to become more aware of their debt to God and the inadequacy of their service to him, and thus the more they do, the less satisfaction they derive from it.

27

Their charity and love makes them want to do so much for God that what they actually do accomplish seems as nothing.

28

These souls humbly and tranquilly long to be taught by anyone who might be a help to them. This desire is the exact opposite of that other desire we mentioned: of those who want to be themselves the teachers in everything.

March

*As Jesus passed along the Sea of Galilee,
he saw Simon and his brother Andrew
casting a net into the sea—for they were
fishermen. And Jesus said to them,
"Follow me and I will make
you fish for people."*
(Mark 1:16–17)

1

There is no reason to marvel at God's granting such sublime and strange gifts to souls he determines to favor. If we consider that he is God and that he bestows them as God, with infinite love and goodness, it does not seem unreasonable.

2

He declared that the Father, the Son, and the Holy Spirit would take up their abode in anyone who loved him [John 14:23]. He takes up his abode in individuals by making them live the life of God and dwell in the Father, the Son, and the Holy Spirit.

3

Such is the activity of the Holy Spirit in the soul transformed in love: The interior acts he produces shoot up flames, for they are acts of inflamed love in which the will of the soul united with that flame, made one with it, loves most sublimely.

4

The same difference that lies between a habit and an act lies between the transformation in love and the flame of love; it is like the difference between the wood that is on fire and the flame that leaps up from it, for the flame is the effect of the fire that is present there.

5

The more intense the fire of union, the more vehemently does this fire burst into flames.

6

The loftier were the words of the Son of God, the more tasteless they were to the impure, as happened when he preached the savory and loving doctrine of the Holy Eucharist; for many turned away [John 6:60–61, 66].

7

Those who do not taste this language God speaks within them must not think on this account that others do not taste it.

8

And the Samaritan woman forgot the water and the water pot because of the sweetness of God's words [John 4:28].

9

Since this soul is so close to God that it is transformed into a flame of love, in which the Father, the Son, and the Holy Spirit are communicated to it, what is so unbelievable about saying that it enjoys a foretaste of eternal life?

10

For on this road there is room only for self-denial (as our Savior asserts) and the cross. The cross is a supporting staff and greatly lightens and eases the journey.

11

If individuals resolutely submit to the carrying of the cross, if they decidedly want to find and endure trial in all things for God, they will discover in all of them great relief and sweetness.

12

I would not consider any spirituality worthwhile that wants to walk in sweetness and ease and run from the imitation of Christ.

13

At the moment of his death he was certainly annihilated in his soul, without any consolation or relief, since the Father had left him that way in innermost aridity in his lower part. He was thereby compelled to cry out: My God, my God, why have you forsaken me? [Matt 27:46].

14

This was the most extreme abandonment, sensitively, that he had suffered in his life. And by it he accomplished the most marvelous work of his whole life surpassing all the works and deeds and miracles that he had ever performed on earth or in heaven.

15

These souls will give their life's blood to anyone who serves God, and they will do whatever they can to help others serve him.

16

They become unhappy and peevish owing to a lack of the consolation they desire to have in spiritual things.

17

Their eyes are fixed only on God, on being his friend and pleasing him.

18

If the inordinate love increases, then, as will be seen, the soul will grow cold in the love of God, and, owing to the recollection of that other love, forget him—not without the feeling of some remorse of conscience. On the other hand, as the love of God increases, the soul will grow cold in the inordinate affection and come to forget it.

19

Through a certain indiscreet zeal they become angry over the sins of others, reprove these others, and sometimes even feel the impulse to do so angrily, which in fact they occasionally do, setting themselves up as lords of virtue.

20

Many of these beginners will make numerous plans and great resolutions, but since they are not humble and have no distrust of themselves, the more resolves they make the more they break, and the greater becomes their anger.

21

Some, however, are so patient about their desire for advancement that God would prefer to see them a little less so.

22

But corporal penance without obedience is no more than a penance of beasts. And like beasts, they are motivated in these penances by an appetite for the pleasure they find in them.

23

Some are very insistent that their spiritual director allow them to do what they themselves want to do....They are under the impression that they do not serve God when they are not allowed to do what they want.

24

In receiving communion they spend all their time trying to get some feeling and satisfaction rather than humbly praising and reverencing God dwelling with them.

25

They cannot bear to hear others being praised without contradicting and undoing these compliments as much as possible.

26

If they do not receive in prayer the satisfaction they crave—for after all it is fit that God withdraw this so as to try them—they do not want to return to it, or at times they either give up prayer or go to it begrudgingly.

27

All her [the bride's] words, thoughts, and works are of God and directed toward him without any of the former imperfections.

28

Everything I do, I do with love, and everything I suffer, I suffer with the delight of love.

29

Even the very exercise of prayer and communion with God, in which she was accustomed to considerations and methods, is now wholly the exercise of love.

30

My beloved, all that is rough and toilsome I desire for your sake, and all that is sweet and pleasant I desire for your sake.

31

This soul indeed, lost to all things, and won over to love, no longer occupies her spirit in anything else.

April

*"Blessed are you when people
revile you and persecute you and utter
all kinds of evil against you falsely
on my account. Rejoice and be glad,
for your reward is great in heaven."*
(Matt 5:11–12a)

1

She even withdraws in matters pertinent to the
active life and exterior occupations for the sake
of fulfilling the one thing the bridegroom said
was necessary [Luke 10:42], and that is attentiveness to God and continual love of him.

2

He also defends the bride in the Song of Songs,
conjuring all creatures of the world, referred to
by the daughters of Jerusalem, not to hinder the

bride's spiritual sleep of love or cause her to awaken or open her eyes to anything else until she desires [Song 3:5].

3

It should be noted that until the soul reaches this state of union of love, she should practice love in both the active and contemplative life.

4

For a little of this pure love is more precious to God and the soul and more beneficial to the Church, even though it seems one is doing nothing, than all these other works put together.

5

Mary Magdalene, even though she was accomplishing great good by her preaching and would have continued doing so, hid in the desert for thirty years in order to surrender herself truly to this love.

6

Since this flame is a flame of divine life, it wounds the soul with the tenderness of God's life, and it wounds and stirs it so deeply as to make it dissolve in love.

7

And the greater the purity, the more abundantly, frequently, and generously God communicates himself.

8

It is noteworthy, then, that love is the soul's inclination, strength, and power in making its way to God, for love unites it with God.

9

The more degrees of love it has, the more deeply it enters into God and centers itself in him.

10

But once it has attained the final degree, God's love will have arrived at wounding the soul in its ultimate and deepest center, which is to transform and clarify it in its whole being, power, and strength, and according to its capacity, until it appears to be God.

11

Christ is little known by those who consider themselves his friends. For we see them going about seeking in him their own consolations and satisfactions, loving themselves very much; but not seeking his bitter trials and death, loving him very much.

12

Nothing created or imagined can serve the intellect as a proper means for union with God.

13

All that can be grasped by the intellect would serve as an obstacle rather than a means if a person were to become attached to it.

14

If fire is to be united with a log of wood, it is necessary for heat, the means to this union, to prepare the log first, through so many degrees of heat, with a certain likeness and proportion to the fire.

15

Now if anyone wanted to prepare the log by an inadequate means, such as air, water, or earth, there would be no possibility of union between the log and the fire.

16

Although truly, as theologians say, all creatures carry with them a certain relation to God and a trace of him (greater or lesser according to the perfection of their being), yet God has no relation or essential likeness to them. Rather, the difference that lies between his divine being and their being is infinite.

17

Intellectual comprehension of God through heavenly or earthly creatures is impossible; there is no proportion of likeness.

18

No creature can serve the intellect as a proportionate means to the attainment of God.

19

God told Moses, who had asked for this clear knowledge, that no one would be able to see him: No one shall see me and remain alive [Exod 33:20]. St. John says: No one has ever seen God or anything like him [John 1:18]. And St. Paul with Isaiah says: Eye has not seen, nor ear heard, nor has it entered the human heart [1 Cor 2:9; Is 64.4].

20

In this mortal life no supernatural knowledge or apprehensions can serve as a proximate means for the high union with God through love.

21

Everything the intellect can understand, the will experience, and the imagination picture is most unlike and disproportioned to God.

22

In order to draw nearer the divine ray, the intellect must advance by unknowing rather than by the desire to know, and by blinding itself and remaining in darkness rather than by opening its eyes.

23

To reach union with God, the intellect must obviously blind itself to all the paths along which it can travel.

24

To be prepared for the divine union the intellect must be cleansed and emptied of everything relating to sense, divested and liberated of everything clearly apprehensible, inwardly pacified and silenced, and supported by faith alone, which is the only proximate and proportionate means to union with God.

25

Many of these beginners want God to desire what they want, and they become sad if they have to desire God's will.

26

They frequently believe that what is not their will, or that which brings them no satisfaction, is not God's will, and, on the other hand, that if they are satisfied, God is too.

27

They are scandalized by the cross, in which spiritual delights are found.

28

Entering by the narrow way of life, about which Christ speaks, is saddening and repugnant to them [Matt 7:14].

29

This night, which as we say is contemplation, causes two kinds of darkness or purgation in spiritual persons according to the two parts of the soul, the sensory and the spiritual.

30

The sensory night is common and happens to many....The spiritual night is the lot of very few.

May

*But I say to you, Love your enemies and
pray for those who persecute
you, so that you may be children of your
Father in heaven; for he makes his
sun rise on the evil and on the good, and
sends rain on the righteous
and on the unrighteous.*
(Matt 5:44–45)

1

Since the condition of beginners in the way of
God is lowly and not too distant from love of
pleasure and of self, as we explained, God desires
to withdraw them from this base manner of
loving and lead them on to a higher degree of
divine love.

2

[God] desires to liberate them from the lowly exercise of the senses and of discursive meditation, by which they go in search of him so inadequately and with so many difficulties, and lead them into the exercise of spirit, in which they become capable of a communion with God that is more abundant and freer of imperfections.

3

It is through the delight and satisfaction they experience in prayer that they have become detached from worldly things.

4

The likeness between faith and God is so close that no other difference exists than that between believing in God and seeing him.

5

Just as there are three Persons in one God, it [faith] presents him to us in this way.

6

Just as God is darkness to our intellect, so faith dazzles and blinds us.

7

Only by means of faith, in divine light exceeding all understanding, does God manifest himself to the soul.

8

People must walk by faith in their journey to God.

9

It is at the time they are going about their spiritual exercises with delight and satisfaction, when in their opinion the sun of divine favor is shining most brightly on them, that God darkens all this light.

10

He leaves them in such dryness that they not only fail to receive satisfaction and pleasure from their spiritual exercises and works, as they formerly did, but also find these exercises distasteful and bitter.

11

Since God puts a soul in this dark night in order to dry up and purge its sensory appetite, he does not allow it to find sweetness or delight in anything.

12

The memory ordinarily turns to God solici-
tously and with painful care, and the soul
thinks it is not serving God but turning back,
because it is aware of this distaste for the things
of God.

13

The lukewarm are very lax and remiss in their
will and spirit, and have no solicitude about
serving God. Those suffering from the purgative
dryness are ordinarily solicitous, concerned, and
pained about not serving God.

14

The reason for this dryness is that God transfers
his goods and strength from sense to spirit.

15

Ordinarily this contemplation, which is secret
and hidden from the very one who receives it,
imparts to the soul, together with the dryness
and emptiness it produces in the senses, an
inclination to remain alone and in quietude.

16

Great wrong would be done to those who possess some degree of this solitary love, as well as to the Church, if we should urge them to become occupied in exterior or active things.

17

She even proclaims how she has acted, and rejoices and glories in having lost the world and herself for her beloved.

18

Those who love are not abashed before the world because of the works they perform for God, nor even if everybody condemns these works do they hide them in shame.

19

Aware of the bridegroom's words in the Gospel, that no one can serve two masters, but must necessarily fail one [Matt 6:24], the soul claims here that in order not to fail God, she failed all that is not God, that is, herself and all other creatures, losing all these for love of him.

20

It should not be held as incredible in a soul now examined, purged, and tried in the fire of tribulations, trials, and many kinds of temptations, and found faithful in love, that the promise of the Son of God be fulfilled, the promise the Most Blessed Trinity will come and dwell within anyone who loves him [John 14:23].

21
However intimate the union with God may be, individuals will never have satisfaction and rest until God's glory appears [Ps 17:15], especially since they now experience its savor and sweetness.

22
It is easy to reach God when all the impediments are removed and the veils that separate the soul from union with him are torn.

23
The death of such persons is very gentle and very sweet, sweeter and gentler than was their whole spiritual life on earth. For they die with the most sublime impulses and delightful encounters of love.

24
The soul has no touch of presumption or vanity, since it no longer bears the leaven of imperfection, which corrupts the mass [1 Cor 5:6; Gal 5:9].

25

As often as God communicated at length with someone, he appeared in darkness.

26

All of this darkness signifies the obscurity of faith with which the divinity is clothed while communicating itself to the soul.

27

When faith reaches its end and is shattered by the ending and breaking of this mortal life, the glory and light of the divinity, the content of faith, will at once begin to shine.

28

Union with God in this life, and direct communication with him, demands that we be united with the darkness in which, as Solomon said [1 Kgs 8:12], God promised to dwell.

29

The [supernatural, spiritual] knowledge is made up of two kinds: distinct and particular knowledge and dark and general knowledge.

30

The distinct and particular knowledge includes four kinds of distinct apprehensions communicated to the spirit without the means of the bodily senses: visions, revelations, locutions, and spiritual feelings.

31

The dark and general knowledge (contemplation, which is imparted in faith) is of one kind only. We have to lead the soul to contemplation.

June

*"And whenever you pray, do not be like
the hypocrites; for they love to stand
and pray in the synagogues and at the
street corners, so that they may be seen by
others. Truly I tell you, they have received
their reward. But whenever you pray,
go into your room and shut the door
and pray to your Father who is in secret;
and your Father who sees in secret
will reward you."*
(Matt 6:5–6)

1

For, as I say, this contemplation is active while
the soul is in idleness and unconcern. It is like
air that escapes when one tries to grasp it in
one's hand.

2

At this time a person's own efforts are of no
avail, but an obstacle to the interior peace and
work God is producing in the spirit through
that dryness of sense.

3

Since this peace is something spiritual and delicate, its fruit is quiet, delicate, solitary, satisfy-
ing, and peaceful and far removed from all the
other gratifications of beginners, which are very
palpable and sensory. For this is the peace that
David says God speaks in the soul in order to
make it spiritual [Ps 85:8].

4

Meditation is now useless for them because
God is conducting them along another road,
which is contemplation and which is very different from the first.

5

Those who walk in the love of God seek neither
their own gain nor their reward, but only to
lose all things and themselves for God; and this
loss they judge to be their gain.

6

She has lost all roads and natural methods in her communion with God, and no longer seeks him by reflections, or forms, or sentiments, or by any other way of creatures and the senses, but she has advanced beyond them all and beyond all modes and manners, and enjoys communion with God in faith and love.

7

A veil is not so thick and opaque that a brilliant light cannot shine through it; and in this state the bond seems to be so tenuous a veil, since it is now very spiritual, thin, and luminous, that it does not prevent the divinity from vaguely appearing through it.

8

It seems to it that the entire universe is a sea of love in which it is engulfed.

9

For God accords to founders, with respect to the first fruits of the spirit, wealth and value commensurate with the greater or lesser following they will have in their doctrine and spirituality.

10

God usually does not bestow a favor on the body without bestowing it first on the soul.

11

Nevertheless, when the wound is made only in the soul without being communicated outwardly, the delight can be more intense and sublime.

12

He who will go to God relying on natural ability and reasoning will not be very spiritual.

13

Our discussion deals only with the supernatural knowledge that reaches the intellect by way of the exterior bodily senses (sight, hearing, smell, taste, and touch). Through these senses, spiritual persons can, and usually do, perceive supernatural representations and objects.

14

Manifestly, these visions and sense apprehensions cannot serve as a means for union since they bear no proportion to God.

15

Meditation is a work of the imagination: for example, the imagining of Christ crucified or at the pillar or in some other scene; or of God seated on a throne with resplendent majesty; or the imagining and considering of glory as a beautiful light, and so on; or in similar fashion, of any other human or divine object imaginable. The soul will have to empty itself of these images and leave this sense in darkness.

16

These considerations, forms, and methods of meditation are necessary to beginners that the soul may be enamored and fed through the senses. They are suitable as remote means to union with God.

17

Yet these means must not be so used that one always employs them and never advances, for then one would never achieve the goal, which is unlike the remote means and unproportioned to it.

18

Many spiritual persons, after having exercised themselves in approaching God through images, forms, and meditations suitable for beginners, err greatly if they do not determine, dare, or know how to detach themselves from these palpable methods.

19
The attitude necessary in the night of senses is to pay no attention to discursive meditation since this is not the time for it. They should allow the soul to remain in rest and quietude even though it may seem very obvious to them that they are doing nothing and wasting time.

20
Through patience and perseverance in prayer, they will be doing a great deal without activity on their part.

21
They must be content simply with a loving and peaceful attentiveness to God, and live without concern, without the effort, and without the desire to taste or feel him.

22
All these desires disquiet the soul and distract it from the peaceful quiet and sweet idleness of the contemplation that is being communicated to it.

23

Those who do not know how to lose themselves, do not find themselves.

24

Strange it is, this property of lovers, that they like to enjoy each other's companionship alone, apart from every creature and all company.

25

The reason they desire to commune with each other alone is that love is a union between two alone.

26

Let us so act that by means of this loving activity we may attain to the vision of ourselves in your beauty in eternal life. That is: That I may be so transformed in your beauty that we may be alike in beauty.

27

All things are yours, and yours mine [John 17:10]. He says this by essence, since he is the natural Son of God, and we say it by participation, since we are adopted children.

28

But they, O my God and my life, will see and experience your mild touch, who withdraw from the world and become mild, bringing the mild into harmony with the mild, thus enabling themselves to experience and enjoy you.

29

Although that which the soul tastes in this touch of God is not perfect, it does in fact have a certain savor of eternal life.

30

It has endured no tribulation, or penance, or trial to which there does not correspond a hundredfold of consolation and delight in this life, and it can say: And pays every debt.

July

*"When you are praying, do not heap up
empty phrases as the Gentiles do;
for they think that they will be heard
because of their many words."*
(Matt 6:7)

1

God then wishes to lead them to more spiritual,
interior, and invisible graces by removing the
gratification derived from discursive meditation.

2

They will no longer taste that sensible food, as
we said, but rather will enjoy another food,
more delicate, interior, and spiritual.

3

The more spiritual they are, the more they discontinue trying to make particular acts with their faculties, for they become more engrossed in one general, pure act.

4

It is sad to see many disturb their soul when it desires to abide in this calm and repose of interior quietude, where it is filled with the peace and refreshment of God.

5

If individuals were to desire to do something themselves with their faculties, they would hinder and lose the goods that God engraves on their souls through that peace and idleness.

6

Any operation, affection, or advertency a soul might desire when it wants to abide in interior peace and idleness would cause distraction and disquietude, and make it feel sensory dryness and emptiness.

7

Contemplation is nothing else than a secret and peaceful and loving inflow of God, which, if not hampered, fires the soul in the spirit of love.

8

In the measure that the fire increases, the soul becomes aware of being attracted by the love of God and enkindled in it, without knowing how or where this attraction originates.

9

Because the enkindling of love in the spirit sometimes increases exceedingly, the longings for God become so intense that it will seem to individuals that their bones are drying up in this thirst.

10

One of the main reasons for the desire to be dissolved and to be with Christ [Phil 1:23] is to see him face to face and thoroughly understand the profound and eternal mysteries of his incarnation, which is by no means the lesser part of beatitude.

11

The first thing the soul desires on coming to the vision of God is to know and enjoy the deep secrets and mysteries of the incarnation and the ancient ways of God dependent on it.

12

There is much to fathom in Christ, for he is like an abundant mine with many recesses of treasures, so that however deep people go they never reach end or bottom, but rather in every recess find new veins with new riches everywhere.

13

One cannot reach in this life what is attainable of these mysteries of Christ without having suffered much.

14

When Moses asked God to reveal his glory, he was told by God that he would be unable to receive such a revelation in this life.

15

True lovers are only content when they employ all that they are in themselves, are worth, have, and receive in the beloved.

16

It ought to be known that God in his unique and simple being is all the powers and grandeurs of his attributes. He is almighty, wise, and good; and he is merciful, just, powerful, and loving.

17

Each of these attributes is a lamp that enlightens it [the soul] and transmits the warmth of love.

18

By means of all the lamps the soul loves each individually, inflamed by each one and by all together, because all these attributes are one being.

19

In this communication and manifestation of himself to the soul, which in my opinion is the greatest possible in this life, he is to it innumerable lamps giving forth knowledge and love of himself.

20

It is noteworthy that the delight the soul receives in the rapture of love, communicated by the fire of the light of these lamps, is wonderful and immense, for it is as abundant as it would be if it came from many lamps.

21

Since these individuals do not understand the mystery of that new experience, they imagine themselves to be idle and doing nothing. Thus, in their struggle with considerations and discursive meditations, they disturb their quietude.

22

They become filled with aridity and trial because of efforts to get satisfaction by means no longer apt.

23

The more they persist at meditation, the worse their state becomes because they drag the soul further away from spiritual peace.

24

They resemble one who abandons the greater for the lesser, turns back on a road already covered, and wants to redo what is already done.

25

They must learn to abide in that quietude with a loving attentiveness to God and pay no heed to the imagination and its work.

26

At this stage, as was said, the faculties are at rest and do not work actively but passively, by receiving what God is effecting in them.

27

Yet it must be kept in mind that, as I explained before, people generally do not perceive this love in the beginning, but they experience rather the dryness and void we are speaking of.

28

They will, in the midst of this dryness and emptiness of their faculties, harbor a habitual care and solicitude for God accompanied by grief or fear about not serving him.

29

A spirit in distress and solicitude for God's love is a sacrifice most pleasing to God.

30

Secret contemplation produces this solicitude and concern in the soul.

31

It will please and comfort one who treads this path to know that a way seemingly so rough and adverse and contrary to spiritual gratification engenders so many blessings.

August

*"Do not store up for yourselves treasures
on earth, where moth and rust consume
and where thieves break in and steal;
but store up for yourselves treasures in
heaven, where neither moth nor rust
consumes and where thieves do not break
in and steal. For where your treasure is,
there your heart will be also."*
(Matt 6:19–21)

1

So God put Moses in the cavern of the rock,
which is Christ, as we said, and showed his
back to him, which was to impart knowledge of
the mysteries of the humanity of Christ.

2

The soul, then, earnestly longs to enter these caverns of Christ in order to be absorbed, transformed, and wholly inebriated in the love of the wisdom of these mysteries, and hide herself in the bosom of the beloved.

3

The reasons the soul desired to enter these caverns was to reach the consummation of the love of God, which she had always been seeking, that is, to love God as purely and perfectly as he loves her.

4

Immensely absorbed in delicate flames, subtly wounded with love through each of them [the lamps of fire], and more wounded by all of them together, more alive in the love of the life of God, the soul perceives clearly that love is proper to eternal life.

5

This feeling, then, of the soul that was once obscure, without this divine light, and blind through the soul's appetites and affections, has now together with the deep caverns of the soul's faculties become not only bright and clear, but like a resplendent light.

6

Inclined in God toward God, having become enkindled lamps within the splendors of the divine lamps, they render the beloved the same light and heat they receive.

7

If at times the soul puts the faculties to work, excessive efforts or studied reasonings should not be used, but it should do so with gentleness and love, moved more by God than its own abilities.

8

Dryness is now the outcome of fixing the senses on subjects that formerly provided satisfaction.

9

As long as one can, however, make discursive meditation and draw out satisfaction, one must not abandon this method.

10

I am not affirming that the imagination will cease to come and go (even in deep recollection it usually wanders freely), but that the person is disinclined to fix it purposely on extraneous things.

11

A person likes to remain alone in loving awareness of God, without particular considerations in interior peace and quiet and repose.

12

When this inability to concentrate the imagination and sense faculties on the things of God proceeds from dissipation and tepidity, there is a yearning to dwell on other things.

13

At the beginning of this state the loving knowledge is almost unnoticeable.

14

The soul is beginning to taste the food of the strong (the infused contemplation of which we have spoken), which in these sensory aridities and darknesses is given to the spirit that is dry and empty of the satisfactions of sense.

15

The first and chief benefit that this dry and dark night of contemplation causes is the knowledge of self and of one's own misery.

16

Now that the soul is clothed in these other garments of labor, dryness, and desolation, and that its former lights have been darkened, it possesses more authentic lights in this most excellent and necessary virtue of self-knowledge.

17

But God also, by means of this dark and dry night of contemplation, supernaturally instructs in his divine wisdom the soul that is empty and unhindered.

18

We conclude that self-knowledge flows first from this dry night, and that from this knowledge as from its source proceeds the other knowledge of God.

19

The dark night with its aridities and voids is the means to the knowledge of God and self.

20

The reason the soul desired to enter these caverns was to reach the consummation of the love of God, which she had always been seeking: that is, to love God as purely and perfectly as he loves her in order to repay him by such love.

21

Lovers cannot be satisfied if they fail to feel that they love as much as they are loved.

22

Just as the soul, according to St. Paul, will know then as she is known by God [1 Cor 13:12], so she will also love God as she is loved by him.

23

Her love for him [God] is as strong and perfect as his love for her, for the two wills are so united that there is only one will and love, which is God's.

24

Insofar as he gives her there his love, he shows her how to love as she is loved by him.

25

Corresponding to the exquisiteness or to the excellence with which the intellect receives the divine wisdom, being made one with God's intellect, is the excellence with which the soul gives this wisdom, for it cannot give it save according to the mode in which it was given.

26

And corresponding to the excellence by which the will is united to goodness is the excellence by which it gives in God the same goodness to God, for it only receives it in order to give it.

27

And according to the excellence of the divine attributes (fortitude, beauty, justice, and so on), which the beloved communicates, is the excellence with which the soul's feeling gives joyfully to him the very light and heat it receives from him.

28

But the more habituated persons become to this calm, the more their experience of this general, loving knowledge of God will increase.

29

It should be known that the purpose of discursive meditation on divine subjects is the acquisition of some knowledge and love of God.

30

The repetition of many particular acts of this loving knowledge becomes so continuous that a habit is formed in the soul.

31

God, too, is wont to effect this habit [of knowledge and love] in many souls, without the precedence of at least many of these acts as means.

September

*"Look at the birds of the air; they neither
sow nor reap nor gather into barns,
and yet your heavenly Father feeds them.
Are you not of more value than they?"*
(Matt 6:26)

1
In the dryness and emptiness of this night of the appetite, a person also procures spiritual humility, that virtue opposed to the first capital vice, spiritual pride.

2
Aware of their own dryness and wretchedness, the thought of their being more advanced than others does not even occur in its first movements.

3

From this humility stems love of neighbor, for they will esteem them and not judge them as they did before.

4

These persons will know only their own misery and keep it so much in sight that they will have no opportunity to watch anyone else's conduct.

5

Since they are aware of their own wretchedness, they not only listen to the teaching of others but even desire to be directed and told what to do by anyone at all.

6

God makes her love him with the very strength with which he loves her.

7

As if he [God] were to put an instrument in her hands and show her how it works by operating it jointly with her, he shows her how to love and gives her the ability to do so.

8

Since God gives himself with a free and gracious will, so too the soul (possessing a will the

more generous and free the more it is united
with God) gives to God, God himself in God;
and this is a true and complete gift of the soul
to God.

9

A reciprocal love is thus actually formed
between God and the soul, like the marriage
union and surrender, in which the goods of
both (the divine essence which each possesses
freely by reason of the voluntary surrender
between them) are possessed by both together.

10

Clearly the soul can give this gift, even though
the gift has a greater entity than the soul's own
being and capacity, for an owner of many
nations and kingdoms, which have more entity
than the owner does, can give them at will to
anyone.

11

This is the soul's deep satisfaction and happiness: to see that it gives to God more than in
itself it is worth.

12

It does this [gives to God more than in itself it
is worth] in heaven by means of the light of

glory and in this life by means of a highly illumined faith.

13

What the soul, therefore, was periodically acquiring through the labor of meditation on particular ideas has now, as we said, been converted into the habitual and substantial, general and loving knowledge.

14

Accordingly the moment prayer begins, the soul, as one with a store of water, drinks peaceably without the labor and the need of fetching the water through the channels of past considerations, forms, and figures.

15

At the moment it recollects itself in the presence of God, it enters on an act of general, loving, peaceful, and tranquil knowledge, drinking wisdom and love and delight.

16

Since it does not obtain the delight it formerly did in its spiritual practices, but rather finds them distasteful and laborious, it uses them so moderately that now perhaps it might fail through defect rather than excess.

17

Nevertheless, God usually imparts to those whom he brings into this night the humility and the readiness, even though they feel displeasure, to do what is commanded of them for his sake alone.

18

Where neither the appetites nor concupiscence reign, there is no disturbance but only God's peace and consolation.

19

In the patience and forbearance practiced in these voids and aridities, and through perseverance in its spiritual exercises without consolation or satisfaction, the soul practices the love of God, since it is no longer motivated by the attractive and savory gratification it finds in its work but only by God.

20

Softened and humbled by aridities and hardships and by other temptations and trials in which God exercises the soul in the course of this night, individuals become meek toward God and themselves and also toward their neighbor.

21

The soul united and transformed in God breathes out in God to God the very divine spiration that God—she being transformed in him—breathes out in himself to her.

22

One should not think it impossible that the soul be capable of so sublime an activity as this breathing in God, through participation, as God breathes in her.

23

How could it be incredible that she also understand, know, and love—or, better, that this be done in her—in the Trinity, together with it, as does the Trinity itself!

24

Because of its obscurity, she calls contemplation night.

25

In contemplation God teaches the soul very quietly and secretly, without its knowing how, without the sound of words, and without the help of any bodily or spiritual faculty, in silence and quietude, in darkness to all sensory and natural things.

26

And how delicately you captivate me and arouse my affections toward you in the sweet breathing you produce in this awakening.

27

And here lies the remarkable delight of this awakening: The soul knows creatures through God and not God through creatures.

28

It should be known that God dwells secretly in all souls and is hidden in their substance, for otherwise they would not last.

29

Yet there is a difference, a great difference, in his dwelling in them. In some souls he dwells alone, and in others he does not dwell alone. Abiding in some he is pleased; and in others he is displeased.

30

He [God] lives in some as though in his own house, commanding and ruling everything; and in others as though a stranger in a strange house, where they do not permit him to give orders or do anything.

October

*"So do not worry about tomorrow,
for tomorrow will bring worries
of its own. Today's trouble is
enough for today."*
(Matt 6:34)

1

It is obvious that these persons at this time necessarily find worldly images dissatisfying.

2

They are of the opinion that the whole matter consists in understanding particular ideas and reasoning through images and forms (the rind of the spirit). Since they do not encounter these images in that loving, substantial quietude, where nothing is understood particularly and in which they like to rest, they believe they are wasting time.

3

The less they understand the further they penetrate into the night of the spirit.

4

Nevertheless, as we mentioned, the imagination usually wanders back and forth during this recollection.

5

In this arid and obscure night the soul undergoes a thorough reform in its imperfections of avarice, in which it coveted various spiritual objects and was never content with any of its spiritual exercises.

6

They become detached from many things because of this lack of gratification.

7

For when the appetites and concupiscences are quenched, the soul dwells in spiritual peace and tranquility.

8

The soul bears a habitual remembrance of God, accompanied by a fear and dread of turning back on the spiritual road.

9

Through perseverance in its spiritual exercises without consolation or satisfaction, the soul practices the love of God.

10

Some spiritual persons call this contemplation knowing by unknowing. For this knowledge is not produced by the intellect that the philosophers call the agent intellect, which works on the forms, phantasies, and apprehensions of the corporal faculties; rather, it is produced in the possible or passive intellect.

11

Yet however sublime this knowledge may be, it is still a dark night when compared with the beatific knowledge she asks for here.

12

It is in that soul in which less of its own appetites and pleasures dwell that he dwells more alone, more pleased, and more as though in his own house, ruling and governing it.

13

It [the soul] does not, however, always experience these awakenings; for when the beloved produces them, it seems to the soul that he is awakening in its heart, where before he remained as though asleep.

14

Oh, how happy is this soul that ever experiences God resting and reposing within it!

15

Although, he is not displeased with other souls that have not reached this union, for after all they are in the state of grace, yet insofar as they are not well disposed, his dwelling is secret to them, even though he dwells in them.

16

But these individuals do not desire or find delight in this [the imagination wandering back and forth]; rather, they are troubled about it on account of the disturbance it brings to that gratifying peace.

17

With the sensory faculties, as we affirmed, one can make discursive meditation, seek out and form knowledge from the objects; and with the spiritual faculties one can enjoy the knowledge received without any further activity of the senses.

18

It is noteworthy that this general knowledge is at times so recondite and delicate (especially when purer, simpler, and more perfect), spiritual, and interior that the soul does not perceive or feel it, even though employed with it.

19

And then this knowledge is still less perceptible when it shines on a purer soul, one freer from the particular ideas and concepts apprehensible by the senses or intellect.

20

For this reason the purer, simpler, and more perfect the general knowledge is, the darker it seems to be and the less the intellect perceives.

21

In observing a ray of sunlight stream through the window, we notice that the more it is pervaded with particles of dust, the clearer and more palpable and sensible it appears to the senses.

22

We also notice that when it [the ray of sunlight] is more purified of these specks of dust it seems more obscure and impalpable to the material eye.

23

The spiritual life has a similar relationship to the intellect, the eye of the soul. This supernatural, general knowledge, and light shines so purely and simply in the intellect and is so divested and freed of all intelligible forms (the objects of the intellect) that it is imperceptible to the soul.

24

This knowledge, when purer, is even at times the cause of darkness because it dispossesses the intellect of its customary lights, forms, and phantasies and effects a noticeable darkness.

25

In these aridities the soul practices corporally and spiritually all the virtues, theological as well as cardinal and moral.

26

David affirms that a person obtains in this night these four benefits: the delight of peace; a habitual remembrance of God, and solicitude concerning him; cleanness and purity of soul; and the practice of virtue.

27

Softened and humbled by aridities and hardships and by other temptations and trials in which God exercises the soul in the course of this night, individuals become meek toward God and themselves and also toward their neighbor.

28

They will no longer become impatiently angry with themselves and their faults or with their neighbor's faults.

29

If they do have envy, it will not be vicious as before, when they were distressed that others were preferred to them and more advanced.

30

The envy they have—if they do have any—is a holy envy that desires to imitate others, which indicates solid virtue.

31

In the midst of these aridities and straits, God frequently communicates to the soul, when it least expects, spiritual sweetness, a very pure love, and spiritual knowledge that is sometimes most delicate.

November

And to the centurion Jesus said,
"Go; let it be done for you according to
your faith." And the servant was
healed in that hour.
(Matt 8:13)

1

Insofar as individuals are purged of their sensory affections and appetites, they obtain liberty of spirit in which they acquire the twelve fruits of the Holy Spirit.

2

For when the sensory delight and gratification coming from things are quenched, neither the devil, nor the world, nor sensuality has arms or power against the spirit.

3

When David declares of this night of contemplation: The night will be my illumination in my delights [Ps 139:11], which is like saying: When I shall delight in the essential vision of God, then the night of contemplation will have changed into day and light for my intellect.

4

The bride knows that now her will's desire is detached from all things and attached to her God in most intimate love.

5

But in this awakening of the bridegroom in the perfect soul, everything that occurs and is caused is perfect, for he is the cause of it all.

6

And in that awakening, which is as though one were to awaken and breathe, the soul feels a strange delight in the breathing of the Holy Spirit in God, in which it is sovereignly glorified and taken with love.

7

When this divine light does not strike so forcibly, individuals apprehend neither darkness, nor light, nor anything at all from heavenly or earthly sources.

8

They will sometimes remain in deep oblivion and afterward will not realize where they were, or what occurred, or how the time passed.

9

While occupying a person's soul, it [this knowledge] renders that soul simple, pure, and clear of all the apprehensions and forms through which the senses and memory were acting when conscious of time.

10

The soul remains, in consequence [in this contemplation], as though ignorant of all things since it only knows God without knowing how it knows him.

11

This forgetfulness occurs only when God abstracts the soul from the exercise of all the natural and spiritual faculties.

12

Because such knowledge does not always occupy the entire soul, this forgetfulness is less frequent.

13

The knowledge we are discussing only requires abstraction of the intellect from any particular, temporal, or spiritual knowledge and an unwillingness to think of either.

14

When, however, there is also a communication to the will, as there almost always is, people will not fail to understand more or less their being occupied with this knowledge if they want to discern this.

15

They will be aware of the delight of love, without particular knowledge of what they love. As a result they will call it a general, loving knowledge.

16

These aridities, then, make people walk with purity in the love of God.

17

Were it not for the satisfaction God himself sometimes infuses, it would be a wonder if the soul through its own diligence could get any sensible gratification or consolation out of its spiritual works and exercises.

18

In this arid night solicitude for God and yearnings about serving him increase.

19

All the imperfections and disorders of the sensory part are rooted in the spirit and from it receive their strength.

20

He [God] leaves the intellect in darkness; the will in aridity; the memory in emptiness; and the affections in supreme affliction, bitterness, and anguish, by depriving the soul of the feeling and satisfaction it previously obtained from spiritual blessings.

21

Through the annihilation and calming of my faculties, passions, appetites, and affections, by which my experience of God was base, I went out from my human operation and way of acting to God's operation and way of acting.

22

United with the divine love, it [my will] no longer loves in a lowly manner, with its natural strength, but with the strength and purity of the Holy Spirit.

23

All the strength and affections of the soul, by means of this night and purgation of the old man, are renewed with divine qualities and delights.

24

This dark night is an inflow of God into the soul that purges it of its habitual ignorances and imperfections, natural and spiritual, and which contemplatives call infused contemplation or mystical theology.

25

Through this contemplation, God teaches the soul secretly and instructs it in the perfection of love without its doing anything or understanding how this happens.

26

When God communicates this bright ray of his secret wisdom to the soul not yet transformed, he causes thick darkness.

27

Because the light and wisdom of this contemplation is very bright and pure, and the soul in which it shines is dark and impure, a person will be deeply afflicted on receiving it.

28

Clearly beholding its impurity by means of this pure light, although in darkness, the soul understands distinctly that it is worthy neither of God nor of any creature.

29

Since the breathing is filled with good and glory, the Holy Spirit, through this breathing, filled the soul with good and glory, in which he enkindled it in love of himself, indescribably and incomprehensibly, in the depths of God.

30

The bride set all this perfection and prepared-
ness before her beloved, the Son of God, with
the desire that he transfer her from the spiritual
marriage, to which he desired to bring her in
this Church Militant, to the glorious marriage
of the Triumphant.

December

Jesus touched her [Peter's mother-in-law] hand, and the fever left her, and she got up and began to serve him.
(Matt 8:15)

1

This communication, consequently, is called a general loving knowledge, for just as it is imparted obscurely to the intellect, so too a vague delight and love is given to the will without distinct knowledge of the object loved.

2

The representation of this light in a more comprehensible and palpable way is not a sign of its greater purity, sublimity, and clarity, as was demonstrated through the example of the ray of sunlight permeated with dust particles and thereby perceptible to the eye.

3

Evidently, as Aristotle and the theologians assert, the higher and more sublime the divine light, the darker it is to our intellect.

4

We were undesirous of leaving this doctrine somewhat more vague than it is. Certainly, I admit that it is very obscure.

5

We did not mean that those beginning to have this general, loving knowledge should never again try to meditate.

6

In the beginning of this state the habit of contemplation is not so perfect that one can at will enter into this act, neither is one so remote from discursive meditation as to be always incapable of it.

7

One can at times in a natural way meditate discursively as before and discover something new in this.

8

Because it seems that God has rejected them, these souls suffer such pain and grief that when God tried Job in this way it proved one of the worst of Job's trials.

9

Clearly beholding its impurity by means of this pure light, although in darkness, the soul understands distinctly that it is worthy neither of God nor of any creature.

10

And what most grieves it is that it thinks it will never be worthy, and that there are no more blessings for it.

11

Since this divine contemplation assails them somewhat forcibly in order to subdue and strengthen their soul, they suffer so much in their weakness that they almost die, particularly at times when the light is more powerful.

12

Both the sense and the spirit, as though under an immense and dark load, undergo such agony and pain that the soul would consider death a relief.

13

How amazing and pitiful it is that the soul be so utterly weak and impure that the hand of God, though light and gentle, should feel so heavy and contrary.

14

This precisely is what the divine ray of contemplation does. In striking the soul with its divine light, it surpasses the natural light and thereby darkens and deprives individuals of all the natural affections and apprehensions they perceive by means of their natural light. It leaves their spiritual and natural faculties not only in darkness but in emptiness too.

15

The bride knows...that her soul is united and transformed with an abundance of heavenly riches and gifts; and that consequently she is now well prepared, disposed, and strong, leaning on her beloved, coming up from the desert of death, flowing with delights, to the glorious thrones of her bridegroom [Song 8:5].

16

The sensory and lower part is reformed, purified, and brought into conformity with the spiritual part.

17

The sensory part not only offers no obstacle to the reception of these spiritual blessings, but is even accommodated to them since it participates according to its capacity in the goods the soul now possesses.

18

May the most sweet Jesus, bridegroom of faithful souls, be pleased to bring all who invoke His name to this glorious marriage.

19

This reception of light infused supernaturally into the soul is passive knowing. It is affirmed that these individuals do nothing, not because they fail to understand but because they understand by dint of no effort other than the receiving of what is bestowed.

20

One should not commingle other more palpable lights of forms, concepts, or figures of meditative discourse, if one wants to receive this divine light in greater simplicity and abundance.

21

What clearly follows is that when people have finished purifying and voiding themselves of all forms and apprehensible images, they will abide in this pure and simple light and be perfectly transformed in it.

22

This light is never lacking to the soul, but because of creature forms and veils weighing on and covering it, the light is never infused.

23

When spiritual persons cannot meditate, they should learn to remain in God's presence with a loving attention and a tranquil intellect, even though they seem to themselves to be idle.

24

For little by little and very soon the divine calm and peace with a wondrous, sublime knowledge of God enveloped in divine love, will be infused into their souls.

25

They should remember that pacification of the soul (making it calm and peaceful, inactive and desireless) is no small accomplishment.

26

Learn to be empty of all things—interiorly and exteriorly—and you will behold that I am God.

27

It remains to be said, then, that even though this happy night darkens the spirit, it does so only to impart light concerning all things.

28

And even though it humbles persons and reveals their miseries, it does so only to exalt them.

29

Only one attachment or particular object to which the spirit is actually or habitually bound is enough to hinder the experience or reception of the delicate and intimate delight of the spirit of love, which contains eminently in itself all delights.

30

Moreover, the soul should leave aside all its former peace because it is prepared by means of this contemplative night to attain inner peace, which is of such a quality and so delightful that, as the Church says, it surpasses all understanding.

31

In this union the soul will love God intensely with all its strength and all its sensory and spiritual appetites. Such love is impossible if these appetites are scattered by their satisfaction in other things.

Bibliography

San Juan de la Cruz: Obras Completas, 2nd ed. Edited with introductions, notes, and revisions of the text by José Vicente Rodríguez; with doctrinal introductions and notes by Federico Ruiz Salvado. Madrid: Editorial de Espiritualidad, 1980.

The Collected Works of St. John of the Cross, 3rd ed. Translated by Kieran Kavanaugh and Otilio Rodriguez; with introduction by Kieran Kavanaugh. Washington, DC: ICS Publications, 1991.

Collings, Ross. *John of the Cross.* The Way of the Christian Mystics, 10. Collegeville, MN: Liturgical Press, Michael Glazier, 1990.

Doohan, Leonard. *The Contemporary Challenge of John of the Cross: An Introduction to His Life and Teaching.* Washington, DC: ICS Publications, 1995.

Foley, Marc, OCD. *John of the Cross: The Ascent to Joy.* Selected spiritual writings; introduced and edited by Marc Foley. New York: New City Press, 2002.

Hardy, Richard P. *John of the Cross: Man and Mystic.* Boston: Pauline Books & Media, 2004.

John of the Cross: Selected Writings. Classics of Western Spirituality. New York/Mahwah, NJ: Paulist Press, 1987.

Matthew, Ian. *The Impact of God: Soudings from St. John of the Cross.* London: Hodder & Stoughton, 1995.

Pacho, Eulogio, OCD. *The Art of Reaching God According to St. John of the Cross: Exposition of the Basic Themes of Sanjuanist Spirituality.* Translated and edited by Augustine Mulloor, OCD. Trivandrum, India: St. Joseph's Press, 1990.

Ruiz, Federico, ed. *God Speaks in the Night: The Life, Times, and Teaching of St. John of the Cross.* Washington, DC: ICS Publications, 2000.

Stein, Edith. *The Science of the Cross.* Translated by Josephine Koeppel. Washington, DC: ICS Publications, 2002.